QWEN 2.5 CO

CODE LIKE A PRO

OLIVER LUCAS JR

TABLE OF CONTENTS

Chapter 5

Chapter 6

Chapter 7

Chapter 8

Chapter 9

Chapter 10

Preface

Welcome to the exciting world of AI-powered coding!

In the rapidly evolving landscape of technology, artificial intelligence is transforming the way we live, work, and interact with the world. One of the most remarkable applications of AI is in the realm of code generation, where machines are learning to write code with increasing proficiency.

This book, "Qwen 2.5 Coder: Code Like a Pro," is your guide to harnessing the power of this cutting-edge technology. Whether you're a seasoned developer or just starting your coding journey, Qwen 2.5 Coder can be your invaluable companion, helping you write code faster, more efficiently, and with greater confidence.

This book is designed with a practical, hands-on approach. We'll explore the core features and capabilities of Qwen 2.5 Coder, guiding you through real-world examples and applications. You'll learn how to generate code in various programming languages, build websites and mobile apps, automate data analysis tasks, and even create simple games.

We'll also delve into advanced techniques like fine-tuning Qwen 2.5 Coder for specific tasks and integrating it with popular development frameworks. Along the way, we'll address ethical considerations and responsible use of AI code generation, ensuring that you're equipped to navigate this transformative technology with awareness and integrity.

By the end of this book, you'll have a solid understanding of how to leverage Qwen 2.5 Coder to enhance your coding skills, boost your productivity, and unlock new possibilities in the world of software development.

So, let's embark on this exciting journey together and discover how Qwen 2.5 Coder can empower you to code like a pro!

Chapter 1

Introduction to Qwen 2.5 Coder

1.1 What is Qwen 2.5 Coder?

Qwen 2.5 Coder is a powerful large language model (LLM) developed by Alibaba Cloud that's specifically designed for coding tasks. Think of it as an AI coding assistant that can understand and generate code in various programming languages. It's part of the Qwen 2.5 family of LLMs, which are known for their strong performance in general language understanding and generation, but Qwen 2.5 Coder has been further trained on a massive dataset of code to excel in the following areas:

Key Capabilities:

Code Generation: Qwen 2.5 Coder can generate code in response to natural language prompts or instructions. For example, you could ask it to "write a Python function to sort a list of numbers" or "create a JavaScript code snippet to validate a form."

Code Comprehension: It can understand the structure and meaning of code, allowing it to analyze existing code, identify potential errors, and even explain how the code works.

Code Translation: Qwen 2.5 Coder can translate code from one programming language to another, which can be helpful for migrating projects or learning new languages.

Code Completion: It can suggest code completions as you type, helping you write code faster and with fewer errors.

Code Repair: Qwen 2.5 Coder can identify and suggest fixes for bugs or errors in your code.

What Makes It Special:

Massive Dataset: It's trained on a massive dataset of 5.5 trillion tokens of code and code-related data, making it one of the largest code-generation models available.

Multilingual Support: Qwen 2.5 Coder supports 92 programming languages, including popular ones like Python, Java, C++, JavaScript, and Go.

Long Context Window: It can handle code with up to 128,000 tokens, allowing it to work with very long and complex codebases.

Open-Source Availability: The 7B parameter version of Qwen 2.5 Coder is open-source, making it accessible to researchers and developers who want to experiment with and build upon it.

Strong Performance: Qwen 2.5 Coder has achieved impressive results on various code-related benchmarks, even outperforming some larger closed-source models in certain evaluations.

How It Can Be Used:

Qwen 2.5 Coder can be used in a variety of ways, including:

Integrated Development Environments (IDEs): It can be integrated into code editors and IDEs to provide intelligent code completion, suggestions, and error detection.

Code Generation Tools: It can be used to build tools that automatically generate code for specific tasks or applications.

Educational Purposes: Qwen 2.5 Coder can be a valuable tool for learning to code, as it can provide examples, explanations, and assistance with coding exercises.

Qwen 2.5 Coder represents a significant advancement in AI-powered coding, and it has the potential to revolutionize the way software is developed.

1.2 Why Use Qwen 2.5 Coder?

1. Ease of Use:

Natural Language Prompts: You can interact with Qwen 2.5 Coder using simple English instructions. No need to be an expert in complex syntax or commands. Just tell it what you want to achieve, and it will try its best to generate the code for you.

Beginner-Friendly Interface: Whether you're using it through an IDE extension, a web interface, or a dedicated coding tool, Qwen 2.5 Coder is designed to be accessible to users with varying levels of coding experience.

2. Increased Productivity:

Faster Code Generation: Qwen 2.5 Coder can automate many repetitive coding tasks, saving you time and effort. Instead of writing every line of code from scratch, you can use Qwen 2.5 Coder to generate code snippets, functions, or even entire programs quickly.

Reduced Errors: Qwen 2.5 Coder can help you avoid common coding mistakes by generating syntactically correct code and offering suggestions for improvement.

3. Learning and Exploration:

Code Examples: Qwen 2.5 Coder can provide you with code examples in various programming languages, helping you learn new concepts and techniques.

Experimentation: It's a safe environment to experiment with different coding approaches and see how Qwen 2.5 Coder interprets your instructions.

Understanding Code: Qwen 2.5 Coder can help you understand existing code by providing explanations and analysis.

4. Accessibility:

Open-Source Option: The availability of an open-source version of Qwen 2.5 Coder makes it accessible to a wider audience, including students, hobbyists, and independent developers.

5. Powerful Capabilities:

Multilingual Support: Qwen 2.5 Coder's ability to work with a wide range of programming languages makes it a versatile tool for various projects.

Long Context Window: Its capacity to handle long code segments makes it suitable for working on complex applications.

Addressing Potential Concerns:

It's also important to acknowledge potential concerns beginners might have:

Over-Reliance: While Qwen 2.5 Coder is a powerful tool, it's essential to emphasize that it's not a replacement for learning fundamental coding concepts. Encourage users to understand the code generated by Qwen 2.5 Coder and use it as a learning opportunity.

Accuracy: Although Qwen 2.5 Coder is highly advanced, it may not always generate perfect code. It's crucial to review and test the code before using it in production environments.

By addressing these points, you can provide a balanced perspective on the benefits of Qwen 2.5 Coder for beginners while encouraging responsible and effective use.

1.3 Setting Up Your Coding Environment

Before you can start coding with Qwen 2.5 Coder, you need to set up your coding environment. Think of this as preparing your workspace and tools. Here's a step-by-step guide to get you started:

Choosing Your Tools

1 Code Editor or IDE: A code editor is where you'll write your code. Some popular options include VS Code, Sublime Text, and Atom. An IDE (Integrated Development Environment) is like a code editor with extra features to help you code more efficiently. Some popular IDEs include PyCharm and IntelliJ IDEA. For beginners, a simple code editor might be a good starting point.

2 Programming Language: Qwen 2.5 Coder supports many programming languages. Python is a popular choice for beginners because it's easy to learn and read. Other popular languages include JavaScript, Java, and C++.

3 Qwen 2.5 Coder Access: You'll need to figure out how to access Qwen 2.5 Coder. It might have a web interface, an API key you need to use, or an extension for your code editor.

Installation and Configuration

1 Install Your Code Editor/IDE: Follow the instructions on the code editor/IDE's website to download and install it on your computer.

2 Install Programming Language Tools: If you need to install a programming language like Python, follow the instructions on its website.

3 Set Up Qwen 2.5 Coder: Follow the instructions provided by Alibaba Cloud to set up Qwen 2.5 Coder. This might involve creating an account, getting an API key, or installing an extension.

Testing Your Setup

1 "Hello, World!": Write a simple program that prints "Hello, World!" to the console. This will test if your environment is set up correctly.

2 Basic Qwen 2.5 Coder Interaction: Try giving Qwen 2.5 Coder a simple task, like generating a Python function to add two numbers. This will test if you can communicate with Qwen 2.5 Coder.

Once you have completed these steps, you'll have a functional coding environment and be ready to start coding with Qwen 2.5 Coder!

Chapter 2

Generating Your First Code with Qwen 2.5 Coder

2.1 Basic Code Generation Techniques

Qwen 2.5 Coder is designed with user-friendliness in mind, even for those who are new to coding. You can communicate with it using natural language, just like you would with another person. Here's a breakdown of the basic steps involved in generating code using Qwen 2.5 Coder:

1 Start with a clear and concise prompt: Imagine you're giving instructions to a friend. The clearer you are, the better they'll understand what you want. Tell Qwen 2.5 Coder exactly what you want the code to accomplish. For instance, instead of a vague request like "write some code," try something specific like "write a Python function that takes two numbers as input and returns their sum."

2 Specify the programming language: Qwen 2.5 Coder is multilingual! But it needs to know which language you want to use. Clearly state the desired programming language in your prompt. For example, you could say "write a JavaScript function to validate an email address."

3 Include all the essential details: If your code has specific requirements, don't hesitate to include them in your prompt. The more information you provide, the better Qwen 2.5 Coder can tailor the generated code to your needs. For example, you might say "write a Python function to sort a list of numbers in descending order."

4 Review and refine the output: Qwen 2.5 Coder is powerful, but it might not always get things perfect on the first try. Carefully review the generated code to ensure it aligns with your intentions and adheres to the best practices of the chosen programming language. If needed, you can always refine your prompt or provide additional instructions to improve the output.

To illustrate, here are a few examples of prompts you can use:

"Write a Python function to calculate the factorial of a number."

"Create an HTML code snippet for a simple webpage with a heading and a paragraph."

"Generate a JavaScript function to validate a password with at least 8 characters, one uppercase letter, and one number."

"Write a C++ program to find the largest element in an array."

The key takeaway is this: the more precise, detailed, and clear your prompts are, the more effectively Qwen 2.5 Coder can generate the code you need. With a little practice, you'll become fluent in interacting with Qwen 2.5 Coder and generating code like a pro!

2.2 Understanding Prompts and Parameters

To truly unlock the power of Qwen 2.5 Coder and generate code like a pro, it's essential to understand how to craft effective prompts and utilize parameters. Think of prompts as the instructions you give to Qwen 2.5 Coder, while parameters are the knobs and dials you can adjust to fine-tune those instructions.

Prompts: Your Guide for Qwen 2.5 Coder

The quality of your prompts has a direct impact on the quality of the code Qwen 2.5 Coder generates. It's like giving directions – the clearer and more specific your instructions, the better the outcome. Here are some key tips for writing prompts that will get you the best results:

Be clear and concise: Avoid ambiguity and use precise language. Instead of a vague request like "Make a website," try something more specific like "Generate HTML code for a website with a navigation bar, a hero image, and three columns of text."

Specify the desired outcome: Clearly state what you want the code to *do*. Instead of "Write some Python," try "Write a Python function to calculate the area of a triangle given its base and height."

Provide context: Give Qwen 2.5 Coder the necessary background information to understand your request. For example, "Generate JavaScript code for a button that, when clicked, changes the background color of the page to blue."

Use examples: Whenever possible, provide examples of the desired code or output. This helps Qwen 2.5 Coder understand your expectations. For example, "Write a Python function similar to this one: `def add(x, y): return x + y`, but for multiplication."

Parameters: Fine-tuning the Code

Parameters give you more control over the code generation process. They allow you to adjust how Qwen 2.5 Coder interprets your prompt and generates the output. Here are some common parameters you might encounter:

Temperature: This parameter controls the "creativity" of Qwen 2.5 Coder. A lower temperature results in more predictable and deterministic code, while a higher temperature allows for more diverse and unexpected outputs.

Max tokens: This sets a limit on the length of the generated code.

Top k: This parameter limits the code generation to the top k most likely tokens at each step, which can help improve the quality and coherence of the output.

Stop sequences: You can define specific sequences of characters that, when generated, will cause Qwen 2.5 Coder to stop generating further code.

By mastering the art of prompt writing and utilizing parameters effectively, you can guide Qwen 2.5 Coder to generate code that precisely meets your needs and preferences.

2.3 Generating Code in Different Programming Languages

One of the most remarkable features of Qwen 2.5 Coder is its ability to generate code in a wide variety of programming languages. This versatility makes it a valuable tool for any programmer, regardless of their preferred language or the specific needs of a project.

Qwen 2.5 Coder's multilingual capabilities stem from its extensive training on a massive dataset of code encompassing many different programming paradigms and syntaxes. This allows it to understand the nuances of each language and generate code that is both syntactically correct and semantically meaningful.

To generate code in a specific language, you simply need to specify the language in your prompt. For example:

Python: "Write a Python function to calculate the Fibonacci sequence."

JavaScript: "Generate JavaScript code for a button that, when clicked, displays an alert message."

Java: "Create a Java class that represents a customer with attributes like name, address, and phone number."

C++: "Write a C++ program to find the prime numbers between 1 and 100."

Go: "Generate Go code for a simple web server that listens on port 8080."

Qwen 2.5 Coder can handle a wide range of languages, including popular ones like:

- Python
- JavaScript
- Java
- C++
- C#
- Go
- PHP
- Ruby
- Swift
- Kotlin
- TypeScript
- And many more!

This multilingual capability opens up exciting possibilities for developers. You can use Qwen 2.5 Coder to:

Learn new languages: See how common programming concepts are expressed in different languages.

Translate code: Convert code from one language to another, which can be helpful for migrating projects or understanding legacy code.

Prototype quickly: Experiment with different languages to see which one is best suited for a particular task.

Work on diverse projects: Contribute to projects that use a variety of languages without needing to be an expert in all of them.

No matter what programming language you prefer or need to use, Qwen 2.5 Coder can be your coding companion, helping you generate code efficiently and effectively.

Chapter 3

Qwen 2.5 Coder for Web Development

3.1 Building Websites with Qwen 2.5 Coder

Qwen 2.5 Coder can generate code in the core languages of the web: HTML, CSS, and JavaScript. This means you can use it to create various website elements, from basic layouts and styling to interactive features and dynamic content.

Here are some ways Qwen 2.5 Coder can help you build websites:

Generate basic HTML structure: Provide a prompt describing the layout you want (e.g., "Create an HTML page with a header, a navigation bar, a main content area, and a footer."), and Qwen 2.5 Coder will generate the basic HTML structure for you.

Create CSS styles: Describe the visual styles you want to apply (e.g., "Make the header background color blue, the text white, and center-align the navigation links."), and Qwen 2.5 Coder will generate the corresponding CSS code.

Add JavaScript functionality: Describe the interactive behavior you want to implement (e.g., "Write JavaScript code to make a button that, when clicked, hides or shows a section of text."), and Qwen 2.5 Coder will generate the JavaScript code for you.

Build forms: Describe the form elements you need (e.g., "Create an HTML form with fields for name, email, and a message, and a submit button."), and Qwen 2.5 Coder will generate the HTML code for the form.

Generate responsive layouts: Specify that you want a responsive design (e.g., "Create a responsive webpage that adapts to different screen sizes."), and Qwen 2.5 Coder will generate HTML and CSS code that adjusts the layout for various devices.

Create website templates: Provide a more comprehensive prompt describing the overall structure and design of a website template (e.g., "Generate a website template for a blog with a header, a sidebar, a main content area for posts, and a footer."), and Qwen 2.5 Coder will generate a basic template for you to customize further.

By using Qwen 2.5 Coder for web development, you can:

Speed up development time: Automate the creation of common website elements and structures.

Reduce errors: Generate syntactically correct code and avoid common mistakes.

Focus on creativity: Spend more time on the design and functionality of your website, rather than the tedious aspects of coding.

Learn new techniques: Explore different ways to implement web features and learn from the code generated by Qwen 2.5 Coder.

In the next section, we'll delve deeper into how Qwen 2.5 Coder can help you generate specific web elements like HTML, CSS, and JavaScript code.

3.2. Generating HTML, CSS, and JavaScript

Qwen 2.5 Coder can be your coding assistant for all three core web technologies: HTML, CSS, and JavaScript. Let's see how it can help you generate code for each of these:

HTML (HyperText Markup Language)

HTML provides the basic structure and content of a web page. Qwen 2.5 Coder can generate HTML code for various elements, including:

Headings: "Create an H1 heading that says 'Welcome to my website!'"

Paragraphs: "Generate a paragraph of text with the following content: 'This is my website. I hope you enjoy it!'"

Links: "Create a link to Google with the text 'Search Google.'"

Images: "Add an image to the page with the source 'images/my-image.jpg' and the alt text 'My Image.'"

Lists: "Generate an unordered list with three items: apples, bananas, and oranges."

Tables: "Create a table with three columns: Name, Age, and City."

Forms: "Generate an HTML form with fields for name, email, and a submit button."

Divisions: "Create a div element with the class 'container' and the id 'main-content.'"

CSS (Cascading Style Sheets)

CSS is used to style the appearance of HTML elements. Qwen 2.5 Coder can generate CSS code to control various aspects of styling, such as:

Colors: "Make the background color of the body blue."

Fonts: "Set the font family of all paragraphs to Arial."

Sizes: "Make the H1 heading 36px in size."

Margins and Padding: "Add a 20px margin to the top and bottom of the main content area."

Borders: "Add a 1px solid black border to the image."

Positioning: "Position the navigation bar at the top of the page with a fixed position."

Responsive design: "Make the layout responsive so that it adapts to different screen sizes."

JavaScript

JavaScript adds interactivity and dynamic behavior to websites. Qwen 2.5 Coder can generate JavaScript code for various purposes, such as:

Handling events: "Write JavaScript code to make a button that, when clicked, changes the text of a paragraph."

Manipulating the DOM: "Generate JavaScript code to add a new list item to an existing unordered list."

Validating forms: "Create a JavaScript function to validate that an email address is in the correct format."

Making API calls: "Write JavaScript code to fetch data from an API and display it on the page."

Creating animations: "Generate JavaScript code to animate a div element from left to right."

By combining its ability to generate HTML, CSS, and JavaScript, Qwen 2.5 Coder can help you create complete and functional website components and even entire web pages. As you become more comfortable with its capabilities, you can use it to tackle increasingly complex web development tasks and bring your website visions to life.

3.3 Creating Interactive Web Elements

Interactive web elements are essential for engaging users and creating dynamic online experiences. Qwen 2.5 Coder can be your partner in bringing these elements to life, generating the necessary code to make your website more responsive and captivating.

Here's how Qwen 2.5 Coder can assist you in creating interactive web elements:

1. Buttons with Dynamic Actions:

Simple Click Events: "Create a button that, when clicked, changes the text of a paragraph to 'Hello, world!'"

Toggle Effects: "Generate code for a button that toggles the visibility of an image when clicked."

Form Submissions: "Write JavaScript code for a button that submits a form and displays a thank you message."

Animations: "Create a button that animates a div element when clicked, moving it across the screen."

2. Interactive Forms:

Input Validation: "Generate JavaScript code to validate a form field, ensuring it's not empty and matches a specific format (e.g., email address)."

Dynamic Form Fields: "Create a form where selecting an option from a dropdown menu dynamically shows or hides additional fields."

Real-time Feedback: "Write code to provide real-time feedback to the user as they fill out a form, such as password strength indicators."

3. Image Sliders and Carousels:

Basic Image Slider: "Generate HTML, CSS, and JavaScript code for a simple image slider that displays a set of images."

Carousel with Controls: "Create a carousel with previous/next buttons and indicators for navigation."

Auto-playing Carousel: "Write code for an image carousel that automatically cycles through images."

4. Interactive Maps:

Displaying Locations: "Generate code to embed a Google Map on a webpage, showing a specific location with a marker."

Interactive Markers: "Create a map with markers that, when clicked, display information about the location in a pop-up window."

Customizable Maps: "Write code for a map that allows users to zoom, pan, and switch between different map styles."

5. Dynamic Content Updates:

AJAX Requests: "Generate JavaScript code to fetch data from a server using AJAX and update a section of the page without reloading."

Real-time Updates: "Create a webpage that displays real-time data, such as stock prices or social media feeds, using websockets."

By utilizing Qwen 2.5 Coder's code generation capabilities, you can create a wide range of interactive web elements that enhance user engagement and make your website more dynamic and enjoyable to use.

Chapter 4

Qwen 2.5 Coder for Data Science

4.1 Automating Data Analysis Tasks

Here's how Qwen 2.5 Coder can help automate your data analysis workflows:

1. Data Cleaning and Preprocessing:

Handling Missing Values: "Write Python code using Pandas to fill missing values in a DataFrame with the mean of the column."

Removing Duplicates: "Generate Python code to remove duplicate rows from a CSV file."

Data Transformation: "Create a Python function to normalize a column of data in a DataFrame."

Data Type Conversion: "Write Python code to convert a column from string to datetime format."

2. Data Analysis and Exploration:

Descriptive Statistics: "Generate Python code to calculate the mean, median, and standard deviation of a column in a DataFrame."

Correlation Analysis: "Write Python code to calculate the correlation between two columns in a dataset."

Data Aggregation: "Create a Python function to group data by a specific column and calculate the sum of another column."

Outlier Detection: "Generate Python code to identify outliers in a dataset using the IQR method."

3. Data Visualization:

Creating Charts and Graphs: "Write Python code using Matplotlib to create a scatter plot of two columns in a DataFrame."

Customizing Visualizations: "Generate Python code to create a bar chart with custom colors and labels."

Interactive Plots: "Create a Python code snippet using Plotly to generate an interactive line chart with zoom and pan functionality."

Generating Reports: "Write Python code to generate a report that includes summary statistics and visualizations of a dataset."

4. Machine Learning Tasks:

Data Preparation: "Generate Python code to split a dataset into training and testing sets."

Model Training: "Write Python code using Scikit-learn to train a linear regression model on a dataset."

Model Evaluation: "Create a Python function to calculate the accuracy of a machine learning model."

Hyperparameter Tuning: "Generate Python code to perform grid search for hyperparameter tuning of a machine learning model."

By automating these data analysis tasks with Qwen 2.5 Coder, you can:

Save time and effort: Focus on the more creative and strategic aspects of data analysis.

Reduce errors: Generate accurate and reliable code for common data analysis tasks.

Improve productivity: Accelerate your data analysis workflows and get insights faster.

Learn new techniques: Explore different approaches to data analysis and learn from the code generated by Qwen 2.5 Coder.

In the next sections, we'll dive deeper into how Qwen 2.5 Coder can be used for specific data science tasks, such as generating code for data visualization and working with popular Python libraries like Pandas and NumPy.

4.2 Generating Code for Data Visualization

Data visualization is a crucial aspect of data analysis, as it helps to communicate insights and patterns in a clear and engaging way. Qwen 2.5 Coder can assist you in generating code for various types of visualizations, making it easier to create compelling charts and graphs from your data.

Here's how Qwen 2.5 Coder can help you generate code for data visualization:

1. Specifying the Visualization Type:

Start by telling Qwen 2.5 Coder what kind of visualization you want to create. Be specific about the chart type, such as:

"Create a bar chart to show the sales of different products."

"Generate code for a scatter plot to visualize the relationship between age and income."

"Write Python code to create a line chart showing the stock price over time."

"Generate a pie chart to display the market share of different companies."

"Create a histogram to visualize the distribution of exam scores."

2. Providing Data and Labels:

Tell Qwen 2.5 Coder what data to use for the visualization and how to label the axes and elements. You can provide the data directly in the prompt or specify a file or data source. For example:

"Use the following data to create a bar chart: `[('Product A', 100), ('Product B', 150), ('Product C', 200)]`. Label the x-axis 'Products' and the y-axis 'Sales'."

"Generate a scatter plot using the data from the file 'data.csv'. The x-axis should be labeled 'Age' and the y-axis 'Income'."

3. Customizing the Visualization:

You can further customize the visualization by specifying details such as colors, titles, legends, and annotations. For example:

"Make the bars in the bar chart blue."

"Add a title to the chart: 'Sales by Product'."

"Include a legend in the scatter plot to distinguish different data points."

"Annotate the highest point in the line chart with its value."

4. Choosing the Library:

Qwen 2.5 Coder can generate code for various data visualization libraries. Specify the library you prefer, such as:

Matplotlib: "Generate Python code using Matplotlib to create a bar chart."

Seaborn: "Write Python code using Seaborn to create a scatter plot with a regression line."

Plotly: "Create a Python code snippet using Plotly to generate an interactive line chart."

5. Generating the Code:

Once you've provided the necessary information, Qwen 2.5 Coder will generate the code for your visualization. You can then copy and paste the code into your project and execute it to create the visualization.

Example:

"Generate Python code using Matplotlib to create a bar chart showing the sales of different products. Use the following data: `[('Product A', 100), ('Product B', 150), ('Product C', 200)]`. Label the x-axis 'Products' and the y-axis 'Sales'. Make the bars blue and add a title to the chart: 'Sales by Product'."

Qwen 2.5 Coder might generate code like this:

Python

```
import matplotlib.pyplot as plt


products = ['Product A', 'Product B', 'Product C']

sales = [100, 150, 200]


plt.bar(products, sales, color='blue')
```

```
plt.xlabel('Products')

plt.ylabel('Sales')

plt.title('Sales by Product')

plt.show()
```

By utilizing Qwen 2.5 Coder's code generation capabilities, you can create a wide range of data visualizations to gain insights from your data and communicate your findings effectively.

4.3 Using Qwen 2.5 Coder with Python Libraries (Pandas, NumPy)

Qwen 2.5 Coder can be a powerful ally when working with popular Python libraries like Pandas and NumPy, which are essential tools for data manipulation and analysis. By understanding how to integrate Qwen 2.5 Coder with these libraries, you can further automate your data science workflows and generate code for more complex tasks.

Pandas:

Pandas is a powerful library for data manipulation and analysis. It provides data structures like DataFrames, which are essentially tables with rows and columns, and offers a wide range of functions for data cleaning, transformation, and analysis.

Here's how you can use Qwen 2.5 Coder with Pandas:

Data Loading: "Generate Python code using Pandas to read a CSV file named 'data.csv' into a DataFrame."

Data Selection: "Write Python code using Pandas to select all rows from a DataFrame where the 'age' column is greater than 30."

Data Manipulation: "Create a Python function using Pandas to add a new column to a DataFrame that calculates the sum of two existing columns."

Data Aggregation: "Generate Python code using Pandas to group a DataFrame by the 'city' column and calculate the average 'income' for each city."

Data Cleaning: "Write Python code using Pandas to fill missing values in a DataFrame with the median of each column."

NumPy:

NumPy is a fundamental library for numerical computing in Python. It provides powerful array objects and a wide range of mathematical functions for operating on these arrays.

Here's how you can use Qwen 2.5 Coder with NumPy:

Array Creation: "Generate Python code using NumPy to create an array of 10 random numbers between 0 and 1."

Array Operations: "Write Python code using NumPy to calculate the dot product of two arrays."

Mathematical Functions: "Create a Python function using NumPy to calculate the sine of each element in an array."

Linear Algebra: "Generate Python code using NumPy to solve a system of linear equations."

Random Number Generation: "Write Python code using NumPy to generate a random sample of 100 numbers from a normal distribution."

Combining Pandas and NumPy:

You can also use Qwen 2.5 Coder to generate code that combines Pandas and NumPy for more advanced data manipulation and analysis. For example:

"Generate Python code using Pandas and NumPy to calculate the mean and standard deviation of each column in a DataFrame."

"Write Python code using Pandas and NumPy to normalize the values in a DataFrame using the z-score method."

"Create a Python function using Pandas and NumPy to calculate the Euclidean distance between two rows in a DataFrame."

Example:

"Generate Python code using Pandas and NumPy to calculate the mean and standard deviation of each column in a DataFrame named 'df'."

Qwen 2.5 Coder might generate code like this:

```python
Python

import pandas as pd

import numpy as np


def calculate_mean_std(df):

    """Calculates the mean and standard deviation
of each column in a DataFrame.
```

```python
    Args:

        df: The Pandas DataFrame.


    Returns:

        A DataFrame with the mean and standard
deviation of each column.

    """

    mean = df.mean()

    std = df.std()

    return pd.DataFrame({'mean': mean, 'std': std})


# Example usage

mean_std_df = calculate_mean_std(df)

print(mean_std_df)
```

By integrating Qwen 2.5 Coder with Pandas and NumPy, you can leverage the strengths of both tools to generate efficient and effective code for a wide range of data science tasks.

Chapter 5

Qwen 2.5 Coder for Mobile App Development

5.1 Building Simple Mobile Apps

While creating complex mobile apps requires in-depth knowledge and expertise, Qwen 2.5 Coder can simplify the process of building basic apps. Here's how it can help:

1. Generating UI Code:

Basic Layouts: "Create a simple Android layout with a TextView and a Button."

List Views: "Generate code for an iOS list view that displays a list of items."

Input Fields: "Write code for a mobile app screen with input fields for username and password."

Navigation Elements: "Generate code for a tab bar navigation in an iOS app."

2. Handling User Interactions:

Button Clicks: "Write code to handle a button click that displays a message on the screen."

Input Validation: "Generate code to validate user input in a form field."

Navigation: "Create code to navigate between different screens in a mobile app."

Data Display: "Write code to fetch data from an API and display it in a list view."

3. Simple App Logic:

Calculations: "Generate code for a simple calculator app that performs basic arithmetic operations."

Data Storage: "Write code to store user preferences in the app's local storage."

Simple Animations: "Create code to animate a button when it's clicked."

Basic Game Logic: "Generate code for a simple game like Tic-Tac-Toe."

4. Platform-Specific Code:

Qwen 2.5 Coder can generate code for both Android (using Java or Kotlin) and iOS (using Swift) platforms. You can specify the platform in your prompt:

Android: "Generate Java code for an Android app that displays a list of contacts."

iOS: "Write Swift code for an iOS app that plays a sound when a button is pressed."

Example:

"Generate Java code for an Android app with a button that, when clicked, displays a toast message saying 'Hello, world!'"

Qwen 2.5 Coder might generate code like this:

Java

```
import android.os.Bundle;

import android.view.View;
```

```java
import android.widget.Button;

import android.widget.Toast;

import androidx.appcompat.app.AppCompatActivity;


public class MainActivity extends AppCompatActivity {


    @Override

        protected void onCreate(Bundle savedInstanceState) {

        super.onCreate(savedInstanceState);

        setContentView(R.layout.activity_main);


            Button button = findViewById(R.id.myButton);

            button.setOnClickListener(new View.OnClickListener() {

        @Override

        public void onClick(View view) {

            Toast.makeText(MainActivity.this, "Hello, world!", Toast.LENGTH_SHORT).show();

        }

    });
```

}

}

By using Qwen 2.5 Coder for mobile app development, you can:

Get started quickly: Generate basic app structures and functionalities without extensive coding knowledge.

Learn mobile development concepts: Explore different mobile development techniques and learn from the code generated by Qwen 2.5 Coder.

Prototype app ideas: Quickly create prototypes of your app ideas to test and refine them.

Focus on design and user experience: Spend more time on the creative aspects of app development while Qwen 2.5 Coder handles the code generation.

In the next sections, we'll delve deeper into generating code for specific mobile platforms and explore how Qwen 2.5 Coder can be integrated with mobile app development frameworks.

5.2 Generating Code for iOS and Android

Qwen 2.5 Coder's ability to generate code for both iOS and Android platforms makes it a versatile tool for mobile app developers. Whether you're building an app for Apple's App Store or Google Play, Qwen 2.5 Coder can assist you in generating the necessary code.

iOS (Swift)

Swift is the modern programming language for iOS app development. Qwen 2.5 Coder can generate Swift code for various iOS components and functionalities:

UI Elements: "Generate Swift code for an iOS button that displays the text 'Click me!'"

Navigation: "Write Swift code to push a new view controller onto the navigation stack."

Data Handling: "Create Swift code to fetch data from an API and display it in a table view."

Animations: "Generate Swift code to animate the size of an image view."

Gestures: "Write Swift code to handle a swipe gesture on a view."

Example:

"Generate Swift code for an iOS button that, when tapped, changes its title to 'Tapped!'"

Qwen 2.5 Coder might generate code like this:

```Swift
import UIKit


class ViewController: UIViewController {


    @IBOutlet weak var myButton: UIButton!


        @IBAction func buttonTapped(_ sender: UIButton) {

        sender.setTitle("Tapped!", for: .normal)

    }
```

```
}
```

Android (Java/Kotlin)

Android app development traditionally uses Java, but Kotlin has gained popularity as a modern and more concise language. Qwen 2.5 Coder can generate code for both Java and Kotlin:

UI Elements: "Generate Java code for an Android TextView that displays the text 'Hello, Android!'"

Activities and Layouts: "Write Kotlin code for an Android activity with a LinearLayout containing two buttons."

Event Handling: "Create Java code to handle a click event on an Android button."

Data Persistence: "Generate Kotlin code to store data in SharedPreferences."

Networking: "Write Java code to make a network request to an API."

Example:

"Generate Kotlin code for an Android app with a button that, when clicked, displays a Snackbar with the message 'Button clicked!'"

Qwen 2.5 Coder might generate code like this:

Kotlin

```kotlin
import android.os.Bundle

import androidx.appcompat.app.AppCompatActivity

import com.google.android.material.snackbar.Snackbar
```

```
import
kotlinx.android.synthetic.main.activity_main.*


class MainActivity : AppCompatActivity() {


    override  fun  onCreate(savedInstanceState:
Bundle?) {

        super.onCreate(savedInstanceState)

        setContentView(R.layout.activity_main)


        myButton.setOnClickListener { view ->

            Snackbar.make(view,  "Button
clicked!", Snackbar.LENGTH_SHORT).show()

    }

  }

}
```

Cross-Platform Considerations:

While Qwen 2.5 Coder can generate code for both iOS and Android, remember that building truly cross-platform apps often requires using frameworks like React Native or Flutter, which allow you to write code once and deploy it on both platforms. Qwen 2.5 Coder can also assist in generating code for these frameworks.

By leveraging Qwen 2.5 Coder's ability to generate platform-specific code, you can accelerate your mobile app development process and create apps for both iOS and Android devices more efficiently.

5.3 Integrating Qwen 2.5 Coder with App Development Frameworks

While Qwen 2.5 Coder can generate code for native iOS (Swift) and Android (Java/Kotlin) development, it can also be integrated with popular app development frameworks. These frameworks offer several advantages, such as cross-platform compatibility, faster development cycles, and code reusability.

Here's how Qwen 2.5 Coder can be used with some of the leading app development frameworks:

1. React Native:

React Native allows you to build mobile apps using JavaScript and React, a popular JavaScript library for building user interfaces. Qwen 2.5 Coder can assist with:

Generating React components: "Create a React Native component for a button that increments a counter when pressed."

Styling components: "Write CSS code to style a React Native text input field."

Handling user input: "Generate JavaScript code to handle a form submission in a React Native app."

Fetching data: "Write JavaScript code using Fetch API to retrieve data from an API in a React Native app."

Navigation: "Generate code for navigating between screens in a React Native app using React Navigation."

2. Flutter:

Flutter uses Dart, a language developed by Google, to build natively compiled applications for mobile, web, and desktop from a single codebase. Qwen 2.5 Coder can help with:

Creating widgets: "Generate Dart code for a Flutter app with a Scaffold and an AppBar."

Building layouts: "Write Dart code to create a Flutter layout with a Row and a Column."

Handling user gestures: "Generate Dart code to handle a tap gesture on a Flutter widget."

State management: "Write Dart code using Provider for state management in a Flutter app."

Animations: "Create Dart code to animate the opacity of a Flutter widget."

3. Ionic:

Ionic is an open-source framework that uses web technologies like HTML, CSS, and JavaScript to build cross-platform mobile apps. Qwen 2.5 Coder can assist with:

Generating UI components: "Create an Ionic component for a list view that displays data from an array."

Styling with CSS: "Write CSS code to style an Ionic button."

Handling user interactions: "Generate JavaScript code to handle a click event on an Ionic card component."

Navigation: "Write JavaScript code to navigate between pages in an Ionic app."

Accessing native device features: "Generate code to access the device's camera using Ionic Capacitor."

Benefits of using Qwen 2.5 Coder with frameworks:

Faster development: Generate code for common UI elements, navigation patterns, and data handling tasks.

Cross-platform compatibility: Write code once and deploy it on multiple platforms (iOS, Android, web).

Reduced code complexity: Frameworks often provide abstractions and pre-built components that simplify development.

Improved code quality: Generate consistent and well-structured code that adheres to framework best practices.

By integrating Qwen 2.5 Coder with app development frameworks, you can combine the efficiency of code generation with the power and flexibility of these frameworks to build high-quality mobile apps more effectively.

Chapter 6

Qwen 2.5 Coder for Game Development

6.1 Creating Basic Game Mechanics

Qwen 2.5 Coder can assist in generating code for fundamental game mechanics, such as:

1. Movement and Collision:

Character Movement: "Generate code to move a character left and right using keyboard input."

Object Collision: "Write code to detect collisions between the player character and obstacles in the game."

Jumping and Gravity: "Create code to make a character jump and fall realistically with gravity."

Projectile Motion: "Generate code for a projectile that moves in a parabolic arc."

2. Scoring and Game State:

Score Tracking: "Write code to keep track of the player's score and display it on the screen."

Game Over Condition: "Generate code to end the game when the player loses all their lives."

Level Progression: "Create code to transition to the next level when the player reaches a certain score."

Saving and Loading: "Write code to save and load the game state, including the player's progress and score."

3. Simple AI:

Enemy Movement: "Generate code for an enemy that moves towards the player character."

Basic Attack Patterns: "Write code for an enemy that shoots projectiles at the player."

Pathfinding: "Create code for an enemy that follows a path to reach the player."

Random Movement: "Generate code for an enemy that moves randomly within a certain area."

4. User Interface (UI):

Displaying Information: "Write code to display the player's health and score on the screen."

Menus and Buttons: "Generate code for a start menu with buttons for starting the game and viewing options."

In-Game HUD: "Create code for a heads-up display (HUD) that shows the player's health, ammo, and other relevant information."

Example:

"Generate Python code using Pygame to move a character left and right using the arrow keys."

Qwen 2.5 Coder might generate code like this:

Python

```python
import pygame


# Initialize Pygame

pygame.init()
```

```python
# Set screen dimensions

screen_width = 800

screen_height = 600

screen = pygame.display.set_mode((screen_width,
screen_height))


# Character settings

character_x = 350

character_y = 400

character_speed = 5


# Game loop

running = True

while running:

    for event in pygame.event.get():

        if event.type == pygame.QUIT:

            running = False


    # Handle movement

    keys = pygame.key.get_pressed()
```

```python
    if keys[pygame.K_LEFT]:
        character_x -= character_speed
    if keys[pygame.K_RIGHT]:
        character_x += character_speed


    # Keep character within screen bounds
    character_x = max(0, character_x)
        character_x = min(screen_width - 50,
character_x)


    # Clear the screen
    screen.fill((0, 0, 0))


    # Draw the character
        pygame.draw.rect(screen, (255, 0, 0),
(character_x, character_y, 50, 50))


    # Update the display
    pygame.display.flip()


pygame.quit()
```

By using Qwen 2.5 Coder for game development, you can:

Experiment with game mechanics: Quickly prototype and test different game mechanics without writing all the code from scratch.

Learn game development concepts: Explore fundamental game development concepts and learn from the code generated by Qwen 2.5 Coder.

Build simple games: Create basic games like platformers, shooters, or puzzle games with the assistance of Qwen 2.5 Coder.

Focus on game design: Spend more time on the creative aspects of game development, such as level design, character design, and storytelling.

In the next sections, we'll explore how Qwen 2.5 Coder can be used to generate code for game logic, AI, and integration with game engines.

6.2 Generating Code for Game Logic and AI

Qwen 2.5 Coder can be a valuable tool for generating code that drives the core logic of your game and creates intelligent opponents or non-player characters (NPCs). This allows you to focus on the creative aspects of game design while Qwen 2.5 Coder assists with the technical implementation.

Game Logic:

Game logic encompasses the rules, mechanics, and behaviors that govern how your game works. Qwen 2.5 Coder can generate code for various game logic elements, such as:

Game Loops and Updates: "Generate code for a game loop that updates the game state and renders the scene every frame."

Input Handling: "Write code to handle player input, such as keyboard presses, mouse clicks, and touch events."

Collision Detection: "Create code to detect collisions between game objects and trigger appropriate actions."

Physics Simulation: "Generate code to simulate basic physics, such as gravity and projectile motion."

Win/Lose Conditions: "Write code to determine when the player wins or loses the game and display the appropriate message."

Artificial Intelligence (AI):

AI in games can create challenging opponents, believable NPCs, and dynamic game experiences. Qwen 2.5 Coder can help generate code for various AI behaviors:

Finite State Machines (FSMs): "Generate code for an enemy AI using a finite state machine with states like 'patrol', 'chase', and 'attack'."

Pathfinding: "Write code to implement A* pathfinding for an enemy that needs to navigate around obstacles to reach the player."

Decision Making: "Create code for an AI agent that makes decisions based on the current game state and player actions."

Learning AI: "Generate code for a simple learning AI that adapts its behavior based on past experiences."

Behavioral Trees: "Write code to implement a behavioral tree for an NPC that performs a sequence of actions based on conditions."

Example:

"Generate code for an enemy AI in a platformer game that patrols a platform and chases the player when they come within a certain range."

Qwen 2.5 Coder might generate code like this (using pseudocode):

```
// Enemy AI

state = "patrol"

patrol_range = 100


function update():

  if state == "patrol":

    // Move back and forth within the patrol
range

    if reached_end_of_patrol:

      reverse_direction()

    move()


    // Check if player is within range

    if distance_to_player < patrol_range:

      state = "chase"


  if state == "chase":

    // Move towards the player

    move_towards(player_position)
```

```
// Check if player is out of range

if distance_to_player > patrol_range:

    state = "patrol"
```

By combining Qwen 2.5 Coder's ability to generate code for game logic and AI, you can create more dynamic and engaging game experiences. You can focus on designing interesting levels, characters, and challenges while Qwen 2.5 Coder assists in bringing those elements to life with interactive and intelligent behaviors.

6.3 Using Qwen 2.5 Coder with Game Engines (Unity, Unreal Engine)

Game engines like Unity and Unreal Engine provide powerful frameworks and tools for building games, and Qwen 2.5 Coder can be integrated with these engines to streamline your development workflow. By combining the strengths of both, you can create more complex and engaging games with greater efficiency.

Unity

Unity is a popular game engine known for its versatility and ease of use. Qwen 2.5 Coder can assist with generating C# code, the primary scripting language for Unity, to implement various game mechanics and features:

Creating Game Objects: "Generate C# code in Unity to create a new GameObject with a Sprite Renderer component."

Controlling Movement: "Write C# code in Unity to move a GameObject using the WASD keys."

Implementing Game Logic: "Create a C# script in Unity to handle player health and damage."

Adding UI Elements: "Generate C# code in Unity to create a button that starts the game."

Working with Animations: "Write C# code in Unity to play an animation when a character jumps."

Example:

"Generate C# code in Unity to make a GameObject rotate when the spacebar is pressed."

Qwen 2.5 Coder might generate code like this:

Code snippet

```
using UnityEngine;


public class RotateObject : MonoBehaviour

{

    void Update()

    {

        if (Input.GetKeyDown(KeyCode.Space))

        {

            transform.Rotate(Vector3.up * 90);

        }
```

```
        }

}
```

Unreal Engine

Unreal Engine is a powerful game engine known for its high-fidelity graphics and realistic physics. Qwen 2.5 Coder can help generate C++ code or Blueprints visual scripting to implement various game elements:

Creating Actors: "Generate C++ code in Unreal Engine to create a new Actor with a Static Mesh component."

Setting up Blueprints: "Create a Blueprint in Unreal Engine that makes a light flicker when triggered."

Implementing Gameplay Mechanics: "Write C++ code in Unreal Engine to implement a player inventory system."

Designing Levels: "Generate code in Unreal Engine to create a simple level with a floor, walls, and a player start location."

Adding Visual Effects: "Write a Blueprint in Unreal Engine to spawn a particle effect when a character takes damage."

Example:

"Generate a Blueprint in Unreal Engine to make a door open when the player overlaps a trigger volume."

Qwen 2.5 Coder could provide a Blueprint setup with the following logic:

1 Trigger Volume: A Trigger Volume component set to overlap events.

2 Door Actor: An Actor with a Static Mesh component representing the door and a Timeline to control the opening animation.

3 Blueprint Script: A Blueprint script attached to the Trigger Volume with the following nodes:

OnActorBeginOverlap: Event triggered when the player overlaps the Trigger Volume.

Cast to PlayerCharacter: Casts the overlapping actor to the PlayerCharacter class.

Play Timeline: Plays the Timeline on the Door Actor to open the door.

Benefits of using Qwen 2.5 Coder with game engines:

Accelerated development: Generate code for common game mechanics, UI elements, and AI behaviors.

Reduced coding errors: Generate syntactically correct and efficient code that adheres to engine best practices.

Focus on creative tasks: Spend more time on designing levels, characters, and gameplay experiences.

Learning game engine features: Explore different engine features and learn from the code generated by Qwen 2.5 Coder.

By integrating Qwen 2.5 Coder with Unity or Unreal Engine, you can amplify your game development capabilities and create more immersive and engaging games.

Chapter 7

Advanced Techniques with Qwen 2.5 Coder

As you become more proficient with Qwen 2.5 Coder, you can explore advanced techniques to further enhance its capabilities and tailor it to your specific needs. Fine-tuning is one such technique that allows you to adapt Qwen 2.5 Coder to excel in particular tasks or domains.

7.1 Fine-tuning Qwen 2.5 Coder for Specific Tasks

Fine-tuning involves taking a pre-trained language model like Qwen 2.5 Coder and training it further on a smaller, more focused dataset. This process allows you to specialize the model for a particular task or domain, improving its performance and accuracy in those areas.

Here's how you can fine-tune Qwen 2.5 Coder:

1 Identify Your Task:

2 Clearly define the specific task or domain you want to fine-tune Qwen 2.5 Coder for. This could be anything from generating code for a specific programming language (e.g., specializing in Python for data science) to generating code for a particular type of application (e.g., web development, game development, mobile app development).

3 Gather a Dataset:

4 Collect a dataset of code relevant to your chosen task or domain. This dataset should be diverse and representative of the types of code you want Qwen 2.5 Coder to generate. The size of the dataset will depend on the complexity of the task and the desired level of performance.

5 Prepare the Data:

6 Format the data appropriately for fine-tuning. This may involve cleaning the data, tokenizing it, and splitting it into training and validation sets.

7 Fine-tune the Model:

8 Use a suitable framework or library to fine-tune Qwen 2.5 Coder on your prepared dataset. This involves adjusting the model's parameters based on the new data, allowing it to learn the specific patterns and nuances of your chosen task or domain.

9 Evaluate the Model:

10 Assess the performance of the fine-tuned model on a separate test dataset. This helps you measure how well the model has adapted to the new task and identify any areas for improvement.

Benefits of Fine-tuning:

Improved performance: Fine-tuning can significantly improve the accuracy and efficiency of Qwen 2.5 Coder for specific tasks.

Customization: Adapt the model to your specific needs and preferences.

Domain expertise: Specialize the model in a particular area, such as a specific programming language or application domain.

Reduced training time: Fine-tuning requires less time and resources compared to training a model from scratch.

Example:

Let's say you want to fine-tune Qwen 2.5 Coder to generate more efficient and idiomatic Python code for data analysis. You could gather a dataset of high-quality Python code for data manipulation, analysis, and visualization using libraries like Pandas and NumPy. Then, you would fine-tune Qwen 2.5 Coder on this dataset, allowing it to learn the best practices and common patterns for data analysis in Python.

By fine-tuning Qwen 2.5 Coder, you can unlock its full potential and create a powerful coding assistant tailored to your specific needs and expertise.

7.2 Working with APIs and External Libraries

Qwen 2.5 Coder's capabilities extend beyond generating code within a single file or project. It can also be used to work with external APIs (Application Programming Interfaces) and libraries, allowing you to integrate your code with a vast ecosystem of online services and functionalities.

APIs:

APIs allow different software systems to communicate and exchange data. Qwen 2.5 Coder can help you generate code to interact with APIs, enabling your applications to access data and services from various sources.

Here's how Qwen 2.5 Coder can assist you in working with APIs:

Making API Requests: "Generate Python code to make a GET request to the GitHub API to retrieve information about a user."

Handling API Responses: "Write JavaScript code to parse the JSON response from an API call and display the data on a web page."

Authentication: "Create Python code to authenticate with an API using an API key."

Error Handling: "Generate code to handle potential errors that may occur during API requests, such as network issues or invalid responses."

API Documentation: "Write code to generate documentation for an API, including descriptions of endpoints, parameters, and response formats."

External Libraries:

External libraries provide pre-built functions and modules that you can incorporate into your code to avoid reinventing the wheel. Qwen 2.5 Coder can help you generate code that utilizes these libraries effectively.

Here's how Qwen 2.5 Coder can assist you in working with external libraries:

Importing Libraries: "Generate Python code to import the Pandas library and read a CSV file into a DataFrame."

Using Library Functions: "Write JavaScript code to use the Lodash library to find the maximum value in an array."

Integrating with Frameworks: "Create Python code to use the Flask framework to build a simple web application."

Working with Databases: "Generate Java code to connect to a MySQL database using the JDBC library."

Machine Learning: "Write Python code to train a machine learning model using the Scikit-learn library."

Example:

"Generate Python code to use the Requests library to make a POST request to an API endpoint with some data."

Qwen 2.5 Coder might generate code like this:

Python

```python
import requests


url = 'https://api.example.com/endpoint'

data = {'key1': 'value1', 'key2': 'value2'}


response = requests.post(url, data=data)


if response.status_code == 200:

    print('Request successful!')

    print(response.json())

else:

    print('Request failed with status code:', response.status_code)
```

Benefits of using Qwen 2.5 Coder with APIs and libraries:

Faster development: Quickly integrate external services and functionalities into your applications.

Reduced code complexity: Leverage pre-built code and avoid writing everything from scratch.

Increased efficiency: Automate tasks related to API interaction and library usage.

Improved code quality: Generate well-structured and reliable code that adheres to best practices.

By harnessing Qwen 2.5 Coder's capabilities to work with APIs and external libraries, you can expand the horizons of your applications and tap into a vast world of online resources and functionalities.

7.3 Debugging and Troubleshooting Code Generated by Qwen 2.5 Coder

While Qwen 2.5 Coder is a powerful tool for generating code, it's important to remember that it's not perfect. Like any code, the code generated by Qwen 2.5 Coder may contain errors or bugs that need to be identified and fixed. This section will guide you through the process of debugging and troubleshooting code generated by Qwen 2.5 Coder.

1. Understand the Code:

Before diving into debugging, take the time to understand the code generated by Qwen 2.5 Coder. Read through it carefully, paying attention to the logic, structure, and syntax. Try to identify any potential areas where errors might occur.

2. Test the Code:

Run the code and observe its behavior. Does it produce the expected output? Are there any error messages or unexpected results? Testing the code will help you pinpoint the areas that need attention.

3. Use Debugging Tools:

Utilize debugging tools available in your code editor or IDE. These tools allow you to step through the code line by line, inspect variables, and identify the source of errors.

4. Analyze Error Messages:

If you encounter error messages, carefully read and analyze them. They often provide valuable clues about the nature and location of the error.

5. Check for Common Errors:

Be aware of common errors that can occur in code generated by language models, such as:

Syntax errors: Typos, missing punctuation, or incorrect use of language constructs.

Logic errors: Flaws in the code's logic that lead to incorrect results or unexpected behavior.

Incomplete code: Missing parts of the code or incomplete implementations of functionalities.

Inefficient code: Code that may work but is not optimized for performance.

Incorrect API Usage: Incorrectly using API parameters or misinterpreting API responses.

6. Refine Your Prompts:

If the generated code consistently contains errors, consider refining your prompts. Be more specific, provide more context, or use examples to guide Qwen 2.5 Coder towards generating more accurate and reliable code.

7. Seek Help and Feedback:

If you're struggling to debug the code, don't hesitate to seek help from online communities, forums, or experienced developers. Share the code, error messages, and your prompt with others to get feedback and assistance.

8. Provide Feedback to Qwen 2.5 Coder:

If you identify errors or areas for improvement in the generated code, consider providing feedback to the developers of Qwen 2.5 Coder. This helps them improve the model and reduce the likelihood of similar errors in the future.

Example:

Let's say Qwen 2.5 Coder generated Python code that produces a `TypeError` because it's trying to add a string to an integer. You could use a debugger to identify the line of code causing the error, inspect the variables involved, and then modify the code to convert the string to an integer before performing the addition.

By following these debugging and troubleshooting techniques, you can effectively identify and resolve issues in code generated by Qwen 2.5 Coder, ensuring that your applications function correctly and efficiently.

Chapter 8

Qwen 2.5 Coder for Code Optimization

8.1 . Improving Code Efficiency

Qwen 2.5 Coder can be a valuable tool for identifying areas where your code can be optimized and suggesting improvements. Here's how it can help:

1. Identifying Performance Bottlenecks:

Analyzing Code Complexity: "Analyze this Python function and identify any potential performance bottlenecks."

Profiling Code: "Generate code to profile this Java application and identify the methods that consume the most time."

Measuring Execution Time: "Write Python code to measure the execution time of this function and suggest ways to improve it."

2. Suggesting Optimizations:

Algorithm Selection: "Suggest a more efficient algorithm for sorting this list of numbers in Python."

Data Structures: "Recommend a more suitable data structure for storing this data in Java."

Loop Optimization: "Optimize this loop in C++ to reduce the number of iterations."

Memory Management: "Identify any potential memory leaks in this JavaScript code and suggest ways to fix them."

3. Refactoring Code:

Simplifying Code: "Refactor this Python code to make it more concise and readable."

Removing Redundancy: "Eliminate any redundant code in this Java program."

Improving Code Structure: "Restructure this C++ code to improve its organization and maintainability."

Applying Design Patterns: "Suggest a suitable design pattern to improve the design of this JavaScript application."

4. Generating Optimized Code:

Efficient Algorithms: "Generate Python code to implement a binary search algorithm."

Optimized Data Structures: "Write Java code to use a HashMap for efficient key-value lookups."

Parallel Processing: "Create C++ code to parallelize this computation using multiple threads."

Asynchronous Operations: "Generate JavaScript code to perform this network request asynchronously."

Example:

"Optimize this Python code for calculating the factorial of a number:"

Python

```
def factorial(n):

    if n == 0:

        return 1

    else:
```

```
return n * factorial(n - 1)
```

Qwen 2.5 Coder might suggest using an iterative approach instead of recursion:

Python

```
def factorial(n):

    result = 1

    for i in range(1, n + 1):

        result *= i

    return result
```

Benefits of using Qwen 2.5 Coder for code optimization:

Improved performance: Create applications that run faster and consume fewer resources.

Enhanced scalability: Build applications that can handle larger datasets and higher workloads.

Reduced development time: Quickly identify and address performance bottlenecks.

Increased code quality: Generate optimized and well-structured code.

By leveraging Qwen 2.5 Coder's capabilities for code optimization, you can create high-performance applications that meet the demands of today's computing environments.

8.2 Refactoring Code with Qwen 2.5 Coder

Refactoring is the process of restructuring existing code without changing its external behavior. It's like reorganizing a room — you're not adding or removing any furniture, but you're rearranging it to improve the layout and make it more functional. Qwen 2.5 Coder can be a valuable assistant in refactoring your code, helping you improve its readability, maintainability, and efficiency.

Here's how Qwen 2.5 Coder can help you refactor code:

1. Identifying Code Smells:

Duplicate Code: "Identify any duplicate code in this Java program."

Long Methods: "Analyze this Python function and suggest ways to break it down into smaller, more manageable methods."

Complex Conditional Logic: "Simplify the nested if-else statements in this C++ code."

Large Classes: "Suggest ways to refactor this JavaScript class to reduce its size and complexity."

2. Suggesting Refactoring Techniques:

Extract Method: "Extract this block of code into a separate method with a descriptive name."

Rename Variable: "Suggest a more informative name for this variable."

Introduce Parameter Object: "Replace this long list of method parameters with a parameter object."

Replace Conditional with Polymorphism: "Refactor this conditional logic using polymorphism."

3. Generating Refactored Code:

Improved Readability: "Refactor this Python code to improve its readability and clarity."

Reduced Complexity: "Simplify this Java code to reduce its cognitive complexity."

Enhanced Maintainability: "Restructure this C++ code to make it easier to maintain and modify."

Increased Reusability: "Extract this common functionality into a reusable module in JavaScript."

4. Applying Code Style Guidelines:

Consistent Formatting: "Format this Python code according to PEP 8 style guidelines."

Naming Conventions: "Ensure that all variables and methods in this Java code follow standard naming conventions."

Code Comments: "Add informative comments to this C++ code to explain its purpose and functionality."

Example:

"Refactor this Python code to extract the calculation logic into a separate function:"

Python

```python
def process_data(data):

    # ... other code ...


    total = 0

    for item in data:
```

```python
        total += item * 2

    # ... other code ...

    return total
```

Qwen 2.5 Coder might generate the following refactored code:

Python

```python
def calculate_total(data):
    total = 0
    for item in data:
        total += item * 2
    return total


def process_data(data):
    # ... other code ...

    total = calculate_total(data)

    # ... other code ...
```

```
return total
```

Benefits of using Qwen 2.5 Coder for refactoring:

Improved code quality: Create code that is easier to read, understand, and maintain.

Reduced technical debt: Address code smells and prevent them from accumulating over time.

Increased productivity: Automate tedious refactoring tasks and focus on more creative work.

Enhanced collaboration: Generate code that adheres to team coding standards and conventions.

By utilizing Qwen 2.5 Coder's refactoring capabilities, you can improve the overall quality and maintainability of your codebase, making it a more valuable asset for your projects.

8.3 Identifying and Fixing Code Smells

Code smells are indicators of potential problems in your code. They are not necessarily bugs, but they can make your code harder to read, understand, maintain, and modify. Qwen 2.5 Coder can help you identify and fix these code smells, leading to cleaner and more efficient code.

Identifying Code Smells

Qwen 2.5 Coder can analyze your code and identify common code smells, such as:

Duplicate Code: Repeated code blocks that appear in multiple places.

Long Methods: Methods that are too long and complex, making them difficult to understand and maintain.

Large Classes: Classes that have too many responsibilities or too much code, violating the Single Responsibility Principle.

Complex Conditional Logic: Nested if-else statements or complex boolean expressions that make the code hard to follow.

Magic Numbers: Unexplained numerical values that appear directly in the code, making it unclear what they represent.

Data Clumps: Groups of variables that often appear together, suggesting they should be encapsulated in a separate class or object.

Feature Envy: Methods that access data from other classes more than their own, indicating potential design flaws.

Fixing Code Smells

Once Qwen 2.5 Coder has identified code smells, it can suggest appropriate refactoring techniques to address them. Here are some common examples:

Extract Method: Extract duplicate code into a separate method to eliminate redundancy and improve reusability.

Split Class: Divide a large class into smaller, more focused classes to improve maintainability and adhere to the Single Responsibility Principle.

Simplify Conditional Logic: Refactor complex conditional statements using techniques like polymorphism, strategy pattern, or guard clauses to improve readability.

Replace Magic Numbers with Constants: Replace magic numbers with named constants to improve code clarity and maintainability.

Introduce Parameter Object: Group related parameters into a separate object to reduce method parameter lists and improve code organization.

Extract Class: Create a new class to encapsulate data clumps and related methods to improve code structure and modularity.

Move Method: Move a method to a more appropriate class to address feature envy and improve object-oriented design.

Example:

Let's say Qwen 2.5 Coder identifies duplicate code in your Python program:

Python

```python
def calculate_area_of_rectangle(width, height):

    return width * height


def calculate_area_of_triangle(base, height):

    return (base * height) / 2


def calculate_area_of_circle(radius):

    return 3.14159 * radius * radius
```

Qwen 2.5 Coder might suggest extracting the calculation logic for each shape into separate functions:

Python

```python
def calculate_area(shape, *args):
```

```python
    if shape == 'rectangle':

        return calculate_area_of_rectangle(*args)

    elif shape == 'triangle':

        return calculate_area_of_triangle(*args)

    elif shape == 'circle':

        return calculate_area_of_circle(*args)


def calculate_area_of_rectangle(width, height):

    return width * height


def calculate_area_of_triangle(base, height):

    return (base * height) / 2


def calculate_area_of_circle(radius):

    return 3.14159 * radius * radius
```

Benefits of using Qwen 2.5 Coder for identifying and fixing code smells:

Improved code quality: Create cleaner, more maintainable, and more efficient code.

Reduced technical debt: Address potential problems early on and prevent them from becoming bigger issues later.

Increased productivity: Automate the process of identifying and fixing code smells.

Enhanced code consistency: Apply consistent refactoring techniques across your codebase.

By leveraging Qwen 2.5 Coder's capabilities for identifying and fixing code smells, you can continuously improve the quality of your code and create a more robust and maintainable software system.

Chapter 9

The Future of Qwen 2.5 Coder and AI Coding

9.1 Emerging Trends in AI Code Generation

1. Enhanced Natural Language Understanding:

Future iterations of Qwen 2.5 Coder are likely to have even more sophisticated natural language understanding capabilities. This means you'll be able to provide more complex and nuanced instructions, and the model will be able to interpret them more accurately. Imagine being able to describe an entire application or feature in natural language, and Qwen 2.5 Coder generating the complete code for you!

2. Multimodal Code Generation:

Multimodal AI, which can process and generate information from various modalities like text, images, and even audio, is gaining traction. In the future, you might be able to provide Qwen 2.5 Coder with a sketch of a user interface or a diagram of a system architecture, and it could generate the corresponding code.

3. Personalized Code Generation:

AI models could learn your coding style and preferences, generating code that aligns with your specific needs and habits. This personalized approach could significantly improve your workflow and productivity.

4. Automated Code Review and Testing:

AI could play a more significant role in code review and testing, automatically identifying potential bugs, security vulnerabilities, and performance issues. This could lead to more robust and reliable software.

5. AI-Powered Code Collaboration:

Imagine collaborating with AI on coding projects, where AI acts as a virtual teammate, suggesting code snippets, completing your code, and even participating in code reviews. This could revolutionize how software is developed.

6. Code Generation for Emerging Technologies:

As new technologies like Web3, blockchain, and the metaverse emerge, AI code generation tools will need to adapt and provide support for these platforms. Qwen 2.5 Coder could be at the forefront of generating code for these exciting new frontiers.

7. Ethical Considerations and Responsible AI:

As AI code generation becomes more powerful, it's crucial to address ethical considerations and ensure responsible use. This includes issues like bias in training data, intellectual property rights, and the potential impact on the developer workforce.

8. Democratization of Coding:

AI code generation tools have the potential to make coding more accessible to a wider audience, including those with limited coding experience. This could empower more people to create software and contribute to the digital world.

By staying informed about these emerging trends and actively participating in the development and responsible use of AI code generation tools like Qwen 2.5 Coder, we can shape a future where AI and humans collaborate to create innovative and impactful software solutions.

9.2 Ethical Considerations and Responsible Use

As AI code generation becomes increasingly powerful and prevalent, it's essential to address the ethical considerations and promote responsible use of these technologies. Here are some key areas to consider:

1. Bias in Training Data:

AI models like Qwen 2.5 Coder are trained on massive datasets of code. If these datasets contain biases, the models may perpetuate or even amplify those biases in the code they generate. This could lead to unfair or discriminatory outcomes. It's crucial to ensure that training data is diverse and representative and to mitigate biases in the training process.

2. Intellectual Property Rights:

Who owns the code generated by AI? This is a complex question with legal and ethical implications. It's important to establish clear guidelines and ownership rights to protect the interests of developers and users of AI code generation tools.

3. Impact on the Developer Workforce:

Will AI code generation tools replace human developers? While these tools can automate certain tasks and improve productivity, they are unlikely to completely replace human developers in the foreseeable future. However, the nature of software development jobs may evolve, requiring developers to adapt and acquire new skills to work effectively with AI.

4. Transparency and Explainability:

It's important to understand how AI models generate code and to be able to explain their decisions. This transparency and explainability are crucial for building trust in AI-generated code and ensuring that it is used responsibly.

5. Security and Safety:

AI-generated code should be secure and safe, free from vulnerabilities that could be exploited by malicious actors. It's important to implement robust security measures and testing procedures to ensure the safety and reliability of AI-generated code.

6. Misuse and Malicious Use:

AI code generation tools could be misused to create harmful or malicious software. It's important to have safeguards in place to prevent such misuse and to promote responsible use of these technologies.

7. Environmental Impact:

Training and running large AI models can have a significant environmental impact due to the energy consumption required. It's important to develop more energy-efficient AI models and consider the environmental footprint of these technologies.

8. Accountability and Responsibility:

Who is responsible for the code generated by AI? It's important to establish clear lines of accountability and responsibility for the development, deployment, and use of AI code generation tools.

Promoting Responsible Use:

Education and Awareness: Educate developers and users about the ethical considerations and potential risks of AI code generation.

Transparency and Explainability: Develop AI models that are transparent and explainable, allowing users to understand how they work.

Bias Mitigation: Implement techniques to mitigate biases in training data and the training process.

Security and Safety: Prioritize security and safety in the development and deployment of AI code generation tools.

Collaboration and Open Dialogue: Foster collaboration and open dialogue among researchers, developers, policymakers, and the public to address ethical concerns and promote responsible use.

By proactively addressing these ethical considerations and promoting responsible use, we can ensure that AI code generation technologies are used for good and contribute to a more equitable and sustainable future.

9.3 The Impact of Qwen 2.5 Coder on the Software Industry

Qwen 2.5 Coder, and AI code generation tools in general, have the potential to significantly impact the software industry in several ways:

1. Increased Productivity and Efficiency:

By automating repetitive coding tasks, Qwen 2.5 Coder can free up developers to focus on more complex and creative aspects of software development. This can lead to faster development cycles, reduced costs, and increased overall productivity.

2. Improved Code Quality:

Qwen 2.5 Coder can help improve code quality by generating code that is consistent, well-structured, and adheres to best practices. It can also assist in identifying and fixing code smells, reducing the likelihood of errors and bugs.

3. Enhanced Accessibility:

AI code generation tools can make coding more accessible to a wider audience, including those with limited coding experience. This could lead to a more diverse and inclusive developer community, with more people able to contribute to the creation of software.

4. Accelerated Innovation:

By automating certain tasks and providing developers with more powerful tools, Qwen 2.5 Coder can accelerate innovation in the software industry. This could lead to the development of new and exciting software applications and services.

5. Evolving Job Roles:

The role of software developers may evolve as AI code generation tools become more prevalent. Developers may need to acquire new skills in areas like prompt engineering, AI model training, and code review to effectively collaborate with AI.

6. New Business Opportunities:

AI code generation is creating new business opportunities in areas like AI model development, code generation tools, and AI-powered software development platforms.

7. Challenges and Concerns:

The rise of AI code generation also presents challenges and concerns, such as the potential for job displacement, the need for ethical guidelines and responsible use, and the risk of over-reliance on AI-generated code.

Overall Impact:

Qwen 2.5 Coder and similar AI tools are poised to revolutionize the software industry, making software development faster, more efficient, and more accessible. While there are challenges to address, the potential benefits are significant, and the future of software development is likely to be shaped by the collaboration between humans and AI.

Specific Impacts:

Startups: Qwen 2.5 Coder can help startups quickly build prototypes and MVPs (Minimum Viable Products) with limited resources, accelerating their time to market.

Large Enterprises: Large companies can use Qwen 2.5 Coder to improve the efficiency of their development teams, reduce costs, and maintain code quality across large projects.

Education: Qwen 2.5 Coder can be a valuable tool for teaching coding concepts and providing students with hands-on experience with AI-powered software development.

Open Source Community: The open-source version of Qwen 2.5 Coder can empower developers in the open-source community to contribute to the development of AI code generation tools and build innovative applications.

By embracing AI code generation technologies like Qwen 2.5 Coder and addressing the associated challenges responsibly, the software industry can unlock new levels of productivity, innovation, and accessibility, shaping a future where software development is more efficient, collaborative, and impactful.

Chapter 10

The Future of Qwen 2.5 Coder and AI Coding

10.1 Finding Support and Documentation

1. Official Documentation:

The first place to look for information is the official Qwen 2.5 Coder documentation provided by Alibaba Cloud. This documentation should provide comprehensive information about the model's features, capabilities, limitations, and usage instructions. It may include:

API documentation: Details about how to interact with the model programmatically.

Tutorials and guides: Step-by-step instructions for common use cases and tasks.

Examples and code snippets: Illustrative examples of how to use Qwen 2.5 Coder in various scenarios.

Release notes: Information about new features, bug fixes, and improvements in each release.

FAQ section: Answers to frequently asked questions.

2. Online Forums and Communities:

Engage with other users and developers in online forums and communities dedicated to Qwen 2.5 Coder or AI code generation in general. These platforms can be valuable resources for:

Asking questions: Get help with specific problems or challenges you encounter.

Sharing knowledge: Share your experiences, tips, and tricks with others.

Finding solutions: Search for answers to common questions or issues.

Staying informed: Keep up-to-date with the latest news, discussions, and developments.

3. GitHub Repository:

If Qwen 2.5 Coder has an open-source version, its GitHub repository can be a valuable resource for:

Accessing the source code: Inspect the code, contribute to its development, or report issues.

Finding examples and demos: Explore examples and demos provided by the community.

Engaging with developers: Interact with the developers and contributors of Qwen 2.5 Coder.

4. Tutorials and Blog Posts:

Look for tutorials and blog posts written by developers and experts who have experience with Qwen 2.5 Coder. These resources can provide valuable insights, tips, and tricks for using the model effectively.

5. Online Courses and Workshops:

Consider enrolling in online courses or workshops that focus on AI code generation or Qwen 2.5 Coder specifically. These can provide structured learning experiences and opportunities to interact with instructors and other learners.

6. Social Media:

Follow Qwen 2.5 Coder or Alibaba Cloud on social media platforms like Twitter or LinkedIn to stay informed about the latest news, updates, and announcements.

By utilizing these resources effectively, you can gain a deeper understanding of Qwen 2.5 Coder, overcome challenges, and unlock its full potential for your coding projects.

10.2 Joining the Qwen 2.5 Coder Community

Connecting with other users and developers within the Qwen 2.5 Coder community can be incredibly beneficial for learning, sharing knowledge, and staying up-to-date with the latest developments. Here are some ways to join and participate in the community:

1. Online Forums and Discussion Groups:

Official Forums: Look for official forums or discussion groups hosted by Alibaba Cloud, where you can interact with other users, ask questions, and participate in discussions.

Community Platforms: Explore community platforms like Reddit, Stack Overflow, or dedicated AI/ML forums where Qwen 2.5 Coder might be discussed. Search for relevant subreddits or tags to find discussions and connect with other users.

2. Social Media:

Follow Alibaba Cloud: Follow Alibaba Cloud's official social media accounts (e.g., Twitter, LinkedIn) to stay informed about news, updates, and announcements related to Qwen 2.5 Coder.

Engage in Hashtags: Use relevant hashtags (e.g., #Qwen25Coder, #AICodeGeneration) on social media platforms to find and participate in conversations about Qwen 2.5 Coder.

3. GitHub Community:

Contribute to the Repository: If Qwen 2.5 Coder has an open-source version, consider contributing to its GitHub repository by reporting issues, submitting bug fixes, or proposing new features.

Engage in Discussions: Participate in discussions and issues on the GitHub repository to share your thoughts, ask questions, or collaborate with other developers.

4. Local Meetups and Events:

AI/ML Meetups: Attend local meetups or events related to AI/ML or software development in general, where you might find other developers interested in Qwen 2.5 Coder.

Hackathons: Participate in hackathons focused on AI or code generation, where you can collaborate with others and build projects using Qwen 2.5 Coder.

5. Online Communities:

Discord Servers: Look for Discord servers dedicated to Qwen 2.5 Coder or AI code generation, where you can engage in real-time discussions, ask questions, and share your experiences.

Slack Channels: Explore Slack channels or workspaces related to AI/ML or software development, where you might find discussions about Qwen 2.5 Coder.

Benefits of Joining the Community:

Learning and Growth: Learn from experienced users, discover new techniques, and expand your knowledge of Qwen 2.5 Coder.

Troubleshooting and Support: Get help with problems or challenges you encounter while using Qwen 2.5 Coder.

Collaboration and Networking: Connect with other developers, share your ideas, and collaborate on projects.

Staying Informed: Stay up-to-date with the latest developments, news, and best practices related to Qwen 2.5 Coder.

By actively participating in the Qwen 2.5 Coder community, you can enhance your learning experience, contribute to the growth of the community, and unlock the full potential of this powerful AI code generation tool.

10.3 Contributing to Qwen 2.5 Coder Development

Contributing to the development of Qwen 2.5 Coder is a fantastic way to give back to the community, improve the model, and learn more about AI code generation. Here are several ways you can contribute:

1. Open-Source Contributions:

If Qwen 2.5 Coder has an open-source version (like the 7B parameter version), you can contribute directly to its development on platforms like GitHub. Here are some ways to contribute:

Report Bugs: If you encounter any bugs or issues while using Qwen 2.5 Coder, report them on the issue tracker. Provide detailed information about the problem, including steps to reproduce it, expected behavior, and actual behavior.

Submit Bug Fixes: If you have the skills to fix a bug, you can submit a pull request with your proposed solution. Make sure to follow the contribution guidelines and coding style of the project.

Propose New Features: If you have ideas for new features or improvements, suggest them on the issue tracker or discuss them with the developers.

Improve Documentation: Help improve the documentation by clarifying existing content, adding new sections, or providing more examples.

Translate Documentation: Translate the documentation into other languages to make it accessible to a wider audience.

2. Data Contributions:

High-quality data is crucial for training and improving AI models. You can contribute by:

Providing Code Samples: Share well-written, diverse, and representative code samples that can be used to fine-tune or retrain Qwen 2.5 Coder.

Creating Datasets: Curate and share datasets of code specifically designed for training code generation models.

Annotating Data: Help annotate existing code datasets with information like function names, comments, or code smells.

3. Feedback and Evaluation:

Provide Feedback: Share your feedback on the model's performance, strengths, and weaknesses. This can help the developers identify areas for improvement.

Participate in Evaluations: Participate in evaluations and benchmark studies to help assess the performance of Qwen 2.5 Coder and compare it to other models.

4. Community Engagement:

Answer Questions: Help answer questions from other users on online forums and communities.

Share Knowledge: Share your knowledge and expertise by writing blog posts, creating tutorials, or giving presentations about Qwen 2.5 Coder.

Organize Workshops: Organize workshops or meetups to teach others about AI code generation and Qwen 2.5 Coder.

Benefits of Contributing:

Improve the Model: Help make Qwen 2.5 Coder a more powerful and useful tool for everyone.

Learn and Grow: Deepen your understanding of AI code generation and contribute to the advancement of the field.

Gain Recognition: Get recognized for your contributions and become a valuable member of the community.

Make an Impact: Contribute to a technology that has the potential to transform the software industry.

By actively contributing to the development of Qwen 2.5 Coder, you can play a part in shaping the future of AI code generation and help create a more efficient, accessible, and innovative software development landscape.